# Table of Contents

Introduction..........2

Chapter 1: Let's Dive into Membership Sites.....5

Chapter 2: Picking the Perfect Membership Site Model........9

Chapter 3: Crafting Your Membership Site's Flavorful Content and Value Proposition......... 13

Chapter 4: Building Your Membership Site...... 16

Chapter 5: Let's Craft Premium Content and Resources........20

Chapter 6: Crafting Your Membership Tiers and Pricing Plans........ 24

Chapter 7: Marketing and Promoting Your Membership Site........ 27

Chapter 8: Let's Keep the Party Going: Retaining and Engaging Members........ 31

Chapter 9: Making Money Moves with Your Membership Site........ 35

Chapter 10: Scaling Your Membership Site Business........ 39

# Introduction

Welcome to "The Ultimate Guide on How To Build and Monetize a Membership Site"! If you're exploring the digital landscape, you've probably come across the buzz around membership sites. They're like this secret club where people share knowledge, expertise, and resources, and guess what? They're not just trendy; they're also incredibly profitable for folks all over the globe. This book? It's your roadmap to understanding everything about membership sites and how to turn them into a thriving online business that keeps the cash flowing.

So, what's the deal with membership sites anyway? Well, think of them as exclusive clubs where creators, experts, and business owners can dish out premium content to a community of like-minded individuals. By creating this kind of VIP environment and offering top-notch stuff, membership sites can reel in devoted members while raking in a steady stream of income. In this guide, we're going to start from square one and gradually move into the nitty-gritty of making serious money with your membership site.

First things first, we'll dive into the different types of membership site models. Then, we'll tackle how to nail down your content and value proposition because, let's face it, if your stuff isn't valuable, no one's going to stick around. Once you've got that sorted, we'll walk you through the process of actually setting up your own membership site. But hold your horses, because just building the site won't cut it. You've got to know how to get the word out there and reel in those members like a pro.

That's where our marketing and promotional strategies come into play. We'll spill the beans on how to attract new members and grow your community like wildfire. Oh, and let's not forget about member retention and engagement—because what's the point of having members if they're not active, right? We'll dish out some killer tips on how to keep them hooked and coming back for more.

Last but not least, we'll talk about the green stuff—money, moolah, cash flow. We'll explore different ways to monetize your membership site, from setting subscription prices to throwing in some upsells and cross-sells to really maximize your profits. Whether you're a one-person show, a small business owner, or a seasoned pro looking to take your online game to the next level, this book has got your back.

Alright, enough chit-chat. Let's roll up our sleeves, dive into the world of membership sites, and turn your dreams of financial freedom into a reality!

# Chapter 1: Let's Dive into Membership Sites

Have you noticed how membership sites have been all the rage lately? It's like they've become the go-to strategy for savvy entrepreneurs looking to not only make money but also cultivate a loyal tribe of followers. So, in this chapter, we're going to unpack what exactly membership sites are and why they're such a game-changer for businesses.

So, what's the deal with membership sites anyway? Well, think of them as exclusive online clubs. You pay a subscription fee, and in return, you get access to all sorts of cool stuff – think exclusive content, resources, and perks that non-members don't get to see.

Now, the beauty of membership sites is that they can cater to pretty much any niche under the sun. Whether you're into fitness, personal development, education, or business, there's bound to be a membership site out there for you. And the content? It can range from online courses and e-books to webinars, forums, and even one-on-one expert advice.

But why should entrepreneurs bother with membership sites when there are so many other ways to make money online? Well, let me break it down for you:

1. **Recurring Revenue:** Picture this: instead of relying on one-off sales, you've got a steady stream of income flowing in every month. That's the magic of membership sites – they provide a predictable source of revenue that lets you sleep easy at night knowing that bills will be paid.
2. **Scalability:** Here's the thing about membership sites – they can grow with you. Unlike a traditional brick-and-mortar business where expansion means more overheads, online membership sites can accommodate thousands of members without breaking a sweat. So, as your tribe grows, so does your bank account.
3. **Community Building:** Ever heard the phrase "strength in numbers"? Well, that's exactly what membership sites offer. By bringing like-minded people together in one virtual space, you're not just selling a product or service – you're creating a community. And let me tell you, loyal communities are worth their weight in gold.
4. **Relationship Building:** Remember that old saying, "It's not what you know, but who you know"? Well, membership sites take that to a whole new level. By fostering ongoing interactions between you and your members, you're not just selling to them – you're building

relationships. And we all know that people buy from people they know, like, and trust.

5. **Market Differentiation:** In a sea of competitors, standing out is key. And that's where membership sites shine. By offering exclusive content and experiences that can't be found anywhere else, you're giving people a reason to choose you over the competition. It's like having a secret weapon up your sleeve.

6. **Authority Building:** Let's face it – in today's crowded online space, credibility is everything. And what better way to establish yourself as an authority in your niche than by running a membership site? By curating top-notch content and resources, you're not just selling products – you're selling expertise.

So, there you have it – the lowdown on membership sites. But wait, there's more! In the chapters to come, we'll be diving deeper into the nitty-gritty of building and monetizing your very own membership site. We'll talk about different models, how to nail down your content strategy, and the steps to launch and promote your site like a pro.

But for now, just remember this: membership sites aren't just a way to make money – they're a way to make a difference. So, let's roll up our sleeves and get ready to change the game together.

# Chapter 2: Picking the Perfect Membership Site Model

## Understanding Membership Site Models

So, you're ready to embark on the journey of building your very own membership site. Congratulations! But before you dive headfirst into the world of content creation and community building, there's a crucial decision awaiting you: choosing the right membership site model.

Think of it as picking the blueprint for your online castle – the model you choose will shape how users access and engage with your content, ultimately influencing the success and profitability of your digital domain. But fear not, for we're here to guide you through the maze of membership site models.

1. All-Access Membership

Picture this: a virtual treasure trove brimming with knowledge, insights, and resources, all yours for the taking. That's the allure of an all-access membership model. Here, members pay a recurring fee for unrestricted entry to your content kingdom, from online courses and e-books to videos and downloadable goodies. It's like having a VIP pass to the ultimate digital buffet, where members can feast on whatever delights their intellectual palate.

## 2. Tiered Membership

Not everyone wants the same banquet spread. Enter the tiered membership model, where variety reigns supreme. With this approach, you can offer different levels of membership, each unlocking a unique array of benefits. Whether it's access to exclusive content, additional features, or personalized support, there's a tier to suit every taste and budget. Plus, it's a savvy way to upsell and cater to diverse audience segments.

## 3. Drip Content Membership

Ever heard the phrase "good things come to those who wait"? That's the ethos behind the drip content membership model. Rather than serving up all your goodies at once, you dole them out gradually over time – think of it as tantalizing teasers released on a weekly or monthly basis. This drip-feed approach keeps members coming back for more, eager to unwrap each new nugget of wisdom.

4. Fixed-Term Membership

Some folks prefer a short-term fling over a long-term commitment – and that's where the fixed-term membership model shines. Here, members pay a one-time fee for access to your content for a set duration. It's perfect for time-bound courses, programs, or events, offering a taste of exclusivity without the strings of a recurring subscription. Think of it as a limited-time offer they simply can't resist.

## Key Factors to Mull Over

Now that you've got a handle on the menu, it's time to consider your dietary preferences I mean, the key factors that'll shape your decision:

**Content Type:** What's on the menu? Determine the type of content you'll be serving up and how it aligns with your audience's cravings.

**Value Proposition:** What makes your content irresistible? Whether it's unlimited access or curated experiences, tailor your model to match your unique selling points.

**Target Audience:** Who's coming to dinner? Get to know your audience inside out – their tastes, preferences, and appetite for engagement.

**Revenue Goals:** What's the bottom line? Consider how each model stacks up in terms of recurring revenue, high-ticket sales, or flash-in-the-pan promos.

**Technical Considerations:** Can your kitchen handle the heat? Assess the technical requirements of each model and make sure your setup can deliver the goods.

## Conclusion

Ah, decisions, decisions. Choosing the right membership site model is no small feat, but armed with insights into your content, audience, and revenue goals, you're well-equipped to make the call. Whether you opt for the all-access buffet, tiered tasting menu, drip-feed delights, or limited-time indulgence, remember to keep your audience's cravings front and center. Next up, we'll unravel the mysteries of defining your membership site's content and value proposition. Bon appétit!

# Chapter 3: Crafting Your Membership Site's Flavorful Content and Value Proposition

So, you've settled on the perfect membership site model – now it's time to infuse it with the delicious content and irresistible value that'll keep members coming back for seconds. Let's dive into the culinary world of defining your membership site's content and value proposition.

## Getting to Know Your Audience

Before you start tossing ingredients into the pot, take a moment to understand who'll be sitting at your digital dinner table. Who are your target audience? What keeps them up at night, and what sets their hearts aflutter? By peeling back the layers of your audience's preferences and pain points, you'll be better equipped to serve up content that hits the spot.

## Crafting Your Unique Selling Proposition (USP)

In a sea of digital offerings, you need a secret sauce that sets your membership site apart. Enter the Unique Selling Proposition (USP) –

your special seasoning that adds flavor and flair to your culinary creation. Is it your secret stash of gourmet recipes, your personalized tableside service, or your bustling community of culinary enthusiasts? Whatever it is, let it shine like a beacon, drawing hungry members to your virtual feast.

## Cooking Up Grade-A Content

Now, onto the main course your content. This isn't just any old buffet; it's a gourmet spread designed to tantalize taste buds and nourish minds. Here's how to whip up a dish that'll have members licking their screens:

1. **Source the Freshest Ingredients:** Dive deep into the pantry of knowledge, scouting out topics and insights that'll leave your members craving more. Keep an eye out for gaps in the market and sprinkle in a dash of innovation to keep things fresh.
2. **Spice Up Your Strategy:** Plot out your content roadmap like a master chef, balancing a variety of flavors and formats. From succulent articles to sizzling videos, cater to every palate with a smorgasbord of options.
3. **Serve Up a Balanced Meal:** Don't just stuff your members full of facts – give them the tools to put their newfound

knowledge into action. Mix in actionable content that empowers members to level up their skills and conquer the culinary world.
4. **Dish Out Exclusivity:** Want to keep members coming back for seconds? Offer up a secret menu of exclusive content, available only to those lucky enough to snag a seat at your table.
5. **Keep the Kitchen Humming:** A great meal is made even better when it's served with a smile. Stay engaged with your members, updating your content regularly and keeping the conversation flowing.

## Stirring Up Engagement

A great meal is best enjoyed with good company – and the same goes for your membership site. Here's how to whip up a side of engagement that'll have members clamoring for a seat at your table:

1. **Set the Scene for Connection:** Create a cozy corner where members can mingle, swap stories, and share their culinary triumphs and tribulations.
2. **Listen, Respond, Repeat:** Be the attentive host who's always ready with a listening ear and a helping hand. Respond to member questions and

feedback promptly, showing them that their voices are heard and valued.

3. **Host an Exclusive Soiree:** Treat your members to a VIP experience with member-only events like live Q&A sessions, workshops, or cooking demos. It's the perfect opportunity to foster deeper connections and stir up excitement within the community.

## In Conclusion

Whew! Crafting your membership site's content and value proposition is no small feat, but with the right ingredients and a dash of creativity, you'll have members lining up around the block. So, roll up your sleeves, sharpen your knives, and get ready to serve up a feast that'll leave members craving more. In the next chapter, we'll fire up the grill and dive into the nitty-gritty of building your membership site from the ground up. Bon appétit!

# Chapter 4: Building Your Membership Site

So, you're ready to dive into the world of membership sites? Buckle up because we're about to embark on a journey to build a kickass online community that'll keep your members coming back for more. In this chapter, we'll break down the essential steps to make your membership site dreams a reality.

## 1. Choosing the Right Platform

Alright, step one: picking the perfect platform. With so many options out there, it's like being a kid in a candy store. But before you get overwhelmed, consider these factors:

- **Technical requirements:** Make sure the platform can handle your needs, from traffic spikes to seamless integration with your existing tools.
- **User experience:** Nobody likes a clunky website. Look for platforms with customizable themes to keep things sleek and user-friendly.
- **Content management:** You need a platform that makes it easy to upload, organize, and protect your content. Bonus points for features like drip content scheduling.
- **Payment and integration:** Smooth sailing on the payment front is crucial. Choose a

platform that plays nice with your preferred payment gateways and other tools.

## 2. Designing Your Membership Site

Now that you've got your platform sorted, it's time to make it look pretty. Here's how:

- **Branding:** Stick to your brand like glue. Use your logo, colors, and fonts to create a site that's uniquely you.
- **Intuitive navigation:** Keep things simple and easy to find. No one wants to play detective to locate your content.
- **Mobile-friendly design:** Don't forget about the small screens! Optimize your site for mobile viewing to ensure everyone can access it on the go.
- **Engaging visuals:** Spruce up your content with eye-catching images and videos. Visuals are key to keeping your members hooked.

## 3. Setting Up Membership Levels and Access

Variety is the spice of life, right? Offer different membership tiers with varying perks to cater to everyone's tastes:

- **Membership tiers:** Give your members options, from basic to premium. Throw in some sweet benefits like exclusive content or discounts to sweeten the deal.
- **Access permissions:** Control who sees what with clear access permissions. Nobody likes stumbling onto a members-only page by accident.

## 4. Testing and Optimizing

Before you hit the big red "launch" button, make sure everything's running like a well-oiled machine:

- **Test, test, test:** Check every nook and cranny of your site for glitches. Get some trusted friends to play guinea pig and give you feedback.
- **Make adjustments:** Take that feedback to heart and tweak your site accordingly. The goal? A seamless user experience from start to finish.
- **Keep optimizing:** Your work isn't done once the site's live. Keep an eye on performance metrics and listen to your members to keep improving.

## Conclusion

And there you have it, folks! Building a membership

site is no small feat, but with the right tools and know-how, you can create something truly special. Choose the right platform, design with flair, offer irresistible membership levels, and never stop fine-tuning. Your members will thank you for it.

# Chapter 5: Let's Craft Premium Content and Resources

Welcome to the creative hub of your membership site journey! Crafting premium content and resources isn't just about filling space—it's the secret sauce that keeps your members hooked and coming back for more. So, in this chapter, we're going to roll up our sleeves and dive into the strategies and best practices for creating content that's not just good, but great.

**Getting to Know Your Audience**

Alright, before we unleash our creativity, let's take a moment to get inside the minds of our audience. Think of them as friends you're trying to impress at a party—you want to know what makes them tick, what keeps them up at night, and what gets them excited. So, do some digging. Research their needs, desires, and pain points. The better you understand them, the easier it'll be to create content that hits home.

**Mixing it Up: Educational vs. Actionable Content**

Now that we've got a handle on who we're

talking to, let's talk about what we're saying. When it comes to content, variety is the spice of life. So, mix it up! Offer a blend of educational content—like tutorials, courses, and webinars—that teach your members something new. But don't stop there. Throw in some actionable content too—stuff like templates, checklists, and step-by-step guides that they can put into practice right away. It's like giving them the theory and the toolbox to go out and conquer the world.

**Keeping it Exclusive and Fresh**

Here's the scoop: exclusivity is your best friend. Your members want to feel like they're part of something special, something they can't get anywhere else. So, give it to them! Offer up exclusive content—industry insights, case studies, insider tips—that's just for them. And don't forget to keep things fresh. Update your site regularly with new and relevant material. Trust me, nothing kills the mood faster than stale content.

**Building Community Through Engagement**

Alright, let's talk about building connections. Your membership site isn't just a place to consume content—it's a community. So, get people talking! Encourage discussions, ask questions, and solicit feedback. Whether it's through forums, live Q&A sessions, or member-exclusive events, create opportunities for your members to interact and engage. After all, a strong community is a happy community.

### Listening and Responding to Your Members

Now, here's the golden rule: listen to your members. Seriously. Pay attention to what they're saying, what they're asking for, and how they're feeling. And when they reach out to you, be there for them. Respond to their queries, address their concerns, and show them that you're listening. It's not just about providing support—it's about building trust.

### Hosting Exclusive Events for Your Members

Last but not least, let's talk about rolling out the red carpet. Hosting member-exclusive events is like throwing a party for your VIPs. Whether it's a webinar, workshop, or even an in-person meetup, these events are all about giving your members something extra. It's a chance for them to connect with each other, learn from industry experts, and take their skills to the next level. Plus, it's a great way to show them how much you appreciate their membership.

## In Conclusion

Phew, we covered a lot of ground! But here's the bottom line: creating premium content and resources isn't just about filling space—it's about adding value. By understanding your audience, offering a mix of educational and actionable content, keeping things exclusive and fresh, fostering engagement, listening to your members, and hosting exclusive events, you're not just running a membership site—you're building a community. And remember, when it comes to content, quality always trumps quantity. So, keep it fresh, keep it relevant, and keep your members coming back for more.

# Chapter 6: Crafting Your Membership Tiers and Pricing Plans

So, you've laid the foundation for your membership site – now it's time to build the framework that'll entice members to come knocking at your digital door. Let's roll up our sleeves and delve into the art of setting up membership tiers and pricing plans that'll have members clamoring for a spot in your exclusive community.

## Getting Inside Your Audience's Head

Before you start slapping price tags on your membership tiers, it's crucial to get inside your audience's head. What makes them tick? What keeps them up at night, scrolling through endless content? Dive deep into the minds of your audience, conducting surveys, engaging in conversations, and dissecting market research like a seasoned detective. The more you understand their desires and pain points, the better equipped you'll be to tailor your membership tiers to their exacting tastes.

## Crafting Irresistible Membership Tiers

Ah, membership tiers – the secret sauce that adds flavor and flair to your offering. Here's how to whip up a menu that'll leave members salivating for more:

1. **A Dash of Differentiation:** Each tier should be like a gourmet dish – distinct, delectable, and packed with flavor. Whether it's exclusive content, personalized coaching, or VIP perks, make sure each tier offers something unique that sets it apart from the rest.
2. **A Pinch of Progression:** Think of your membership tiers as a culinary journey – start with the appetizer and gradually work your way up to the main course. Offer a clear path of progression, enticing members to upgrade as they savor the tantalizing benefits of each tier.
3. **A Sprinkle of Scalability:** As your membership base grows, you'll need a kitchen that can handle the heat. Make sure your membership tiers are scalable, capable of accommodating new members without sacrificing quality or flavor.

## Mastering the Art of Pricing

Now, let's talk turkey – pricing. Here's how to set the right price tag that'll have members reaching for their wallets:

1. **Value-Based Pricing:** What's on the menu is just as important as how much it costs. Set your prices based on the value you provide, considering factors like the exclusivity of your content, the depth of your expertise, and the results members can expect to achieve.
2. **A Taste of Competition:** Take a peek over the neighbor's fence and see what they're serving up. Research what other membership sites in your niche are charging and position your pricing accordingly. Just be sure not to undercut yourself – you're worth more than you think!
3. **A Dash of Promotion:** Sometimes, a little sprinkle of promotion is all it takes to get the party started. Offer time-limited discounts or special bonuses to create a buzz and entice new members to take a seat at your table.
4. **Stirring the Pot:** Pricing is an art, not a science – so don't be afraid to experiment. Test different pricing strategies, gather feedback from your members, and fine-tune your approach until you find the perfect balance that keeps both your revenue and your members happy.

## Communication is Key

Once you've whipped up your membership tiers and pricing plans, it's time to dish them out to your audience. Be transparent about what each tier offers and why it's worth the investment. Transparency builds trust, helping potential members understand the value they'll receive and nudging them closer to hitting that "Join Now" button.

## In Conclusion

Crafting your membership tiers and pricing plans is an art form – one that requires a deep understanding of your audience, a pinch of creativity, and a dash of experimentation. By offering differentiated tiers, setting prices that reflect the value you provide, and communicating transparently with your audience, you'll create a recipe for success that'll have members lining up around the block. So, grab your apron and get cooking – your exclusive community awaits!

# Chapter 7: Marketing and Promoting Your Membership Site

Alright, folks, it's showtime! We're diving deep into the world of marketing and promotion to make sure your membership site doesn't just exist—it thrives. Get ready to roll up your sleeves and dive into some seriously effective strategies to attract and keep those members coming back for more.

## Understanding Your Target Audience

Before we even think about slapping up some ads or sending out emails, let's get to know the stars of the show: your audience. Who are they? What keeps them up at night? What gets them excited? We're talking demographics, interests, pain points—the whole nine yards. Once you've got that down, it's time to create some buyer personas to really get into their heads. This way, you can tailor your marketing messages to hit them right in the feels and offer solutions they can't resist.

## Creating a Marketing Plan

Now that we've got our audience in our sights, it's time to map out our battle plan. Here's the rundown:

1. **Define your goals:** What are you trying to achieve? Whether it's snagging new members, boosting engagement, or raking in the cash, make sure your goals are crystal clear.
2. **Identify your unique selling proposition:** What makes your membership site stand out from the crowd? Shout it from the rooftops and let the world know why you're the best in the biz.
3. **Select marketing channels and tactics:** Time to get creative! From content marketing to social media ads to good old-fashioned SEO, pick the strategies that'll get you the most bang for your buck.
4. **Develop compelling content:** Content is king, baby. Whip up some killer blog posts, videos, podcasts—whatever floats your boat—to show off your expertise and reel in those members.
5. **Implement lead generation strategies:** Let's get those leads rolling in! Offer up some irresistible freebies to entice potential members to hand over their deets.
6. **Leverage social media:** Get social and start mingling with your audience where they hang out online. Share valuable content, sneak peeks, and exclusive offers to get them hooked.
7. **Collaborate with influencers:**

Sometimes it pays to rub elbows with the big shots. Partner up with influencers in your niche to expand your reach and lend some street cred to your site.

8. **Utilize email marketing:** Don't forget about the good old inbox! Keep your subscribers in the loop with regular newsletters, updates, and special offers.
9. **Measure and analyze your results:** Time to put on your detective hat and dig into the data. Keep an eye on your key metrics to see what's working and what's not, then adjust accordingly.

## Engaging Existing Members

But wait, we're not done yet! It's not just about snagging new members—it's about keeping them around for the long haul. Here's how:

- **Keep the goodies coming:** Serve up fresh, exclusive content that keeps your members coming back for more.
- **Build a community:** Get your members talking and interacting with each other through forums, social media groups, or your own member portal.
- **Be responsive:** Don't leave your members hanging! Be quick to respond to their questions, feedback, and comments to show you care.

- **Host events:** Throw some exclusive shindigs like webinars or workshops to keep things interesting and give your members a chance to connect.
- **Show some love:** Recognize and reward your members' loyalty with special perks, discounts, or shoutouts.

## Conclusion

And there you have it, folks! Marketing and promoting your membership site isn't just about shouting into the void—it's about getting to know your audience, crafting a killer plan, and keeping the party going for your members. So go ahead, dive in, and watch your membership site soar to new heights!

# Chapter 8: Let's Keep the Party Going: Retaining and Engaging Members

Alright, folks, it's time to talk about the glue that holds your membership site together: member retention and engagement. Think of it like tending to a garden—you've got to nurture those relationships if you want your community to flourish. So, grab your watering can, because in this chapter, we're diving into the strategies and best practices to keep your members happy, engaged, and coming back for more.

## Why Retention is King

First things first, let's talk about why retention matters. Picture this: it's way easier (and cheaper) to keep the members you've already got than to go out and find new ones. Plus, loyal members are like your personal hype squad—they'll sing your praises to anyone who'll listen. So, by focusing on retention, you're not just keeping the lights on—you're building a tribe of die-hard fans.

1.  Slay with Stellar Content

Alright, here's the golden rule: content is king.

But not just any content—top-notch, drool-worthy stuff that your members can't get enough of. So, do your homework. Figure out what makes your audience tick, what keeps them up at night, and then serve up the goods. And hey, don't be afraid to ask for feedback. Surveys, polls, carrier pigeons—whatever it takes to make sure you're hitting the mark.

2. Build a Tight-Knit Community

Now, let's talk about building bonds. Your membership site isn't just a place to consume content—it's a family reunion waiting to happen. So, roll out the welcome mat. Encourage discussions, foster collaborations, and create opportunities for your members to connect. Whether it's through forums, live events, or carrier pigeon conventions, give them a space to share their stories and support each other.

3. Show Some Love

Alright, let's talk about the L word: love. Active engagement with your members isn't just a nicety—it's a necessity. So, be there for them. Respond to their questions, comments, and carrier pigeon deliveries promptly and enthusiastically. Show them that you care about their success and that you're willing to roll up your sleeves and help them achieve it.

4. Give Props Where Props are Due

Everybody loves a pat on the back, right? So, why not give your members the recognition they deserve? Whether it's through badges, shoutouts, or carrier pigeon medals of honor, acknowledge their achievements publicly. Trust me, a little recognition goes a long way in keeping your members engaged and motivated.

5. Roll Out the Red Carpet

Now, let's talk about perks. Exclusive benefits like early access to content, discounts on partner products, or carrier pigeon valet services can go a long way in keeping your members happy and engaged. So, don't be afraid to spoil them a little. After all, they're the lifeblood of your community.

6. Keep on Innovating

Alright, let's talk about staying ahead of the curve. Your membership site isn't a set-it-and-forget-it kind of deal—it's a living, breathing organism that needs constant TLC. So, keep your finger on the pulse. Regularly assess what's working, what's not, and what could use a little sprucing up. And don't forget to ask your members for their input. After all, they're the ones who know best.

7. Keep Tabs on the Crowd

Alright, let's talk about keeping an eye on things. Analytics and tracking tools are your best friends when it comes to monitoring member behavior. So, keep tabs on who's logging in, what they're clicking on, and whether they're bringing carrier pigeons to the party. Identify any red flags early on and swoop in with personalized interventions to keep your members on board.

8. Let Your Members Call the Shots

Last but not least, let's talk about democracy. Your members aren't just passengers on this journey—they're co-pilots. So, give them a voice. Regularly solicit feedback through surveys, polls, or carrier pigeon focus groups, and then act on it. Implement the changes they're asking for and keep them in the loop every step of the way.

## In Conclusion

Phew, that was a lot of ground to cover! But

here's the bottom line: retaining and engaging your members isn't just about keeping the lights on—it's about building a thriving community. So, keep serving up killer content, building bonds, showing your love, giving props where props are due, rolling out the red carpet, staying ahead of the curve, keeping tabs on the crowd, and letting your members call the shots. After all, they're the ones who make the magic happen.

# Chapter 9: Making Money Moves with Your Membership Site

Alright, let's talk turkey – monetizing your membership site is the bread and butter of keeping your business afloat. In this chapter, we'll dive deep into the treasure trove of strategies and techniques to turn your membership site into a cash cow.

### 1. Membership Fees: The Bedrock of Revenue

First things first – membership fees. This is the bread and butter of monetizing your site. Whether you're running an All-Access, Tiered, Drip Content, or Fixed-Term model, charging membership fees is your golden ticket to a steady stream of income. From monthly subscriptions to one-time access fees, there's a plethora of options to suit your audience's appetite and your business's bottom line.

### 2. Upselling and Cross-Selling: Adding Flavor to the Mix

Now, let's kick things up a notch with a dash of upselling and cross-selling. Upselling is like offering dessert after a satisfying meal – it entices members to indulge in higher-priced tiers or premium features, boosting their lifetime value to your business. Meanwhile, cross-selling is like recommending the perfect wine to complement their meal – it involves promoting related products or services to your members, adding value to their membership experience while padding your pockets with additional revenue.

### 3. Affiliate Marketing: Partnering for Profit

Ever heard the phrase "strength in numbers"? That's the ethos behind affiliate marketing. By teaming up with relevant brands and businesses, you can promote their products or services to your members in exchange for a juicy commission on each sale. Just be sure to choose your partners wisely – maintaining trust with your members is paramount to your long-term success.

### 4. Sponsored Content and Advertisements: Monetization with a Twist

For some extra flavor, consider incorporating sponsored content and advertisements into the mix. Partnering with brands to create tailored content or promoting their products to your members can add a tasty revenue stream to your plate. But remember – moderation is key. Too many ads can leave a bitter taste in your members' mouths, so be sure to strike a balance between monetization and user experience.

### 5. Product and Service Launches: Serving Up Your Specialties

Last but not least, leverage your membership site as a platform for launching and selling your own products or services. From e-books and courses to workshops and consulting services, your expertise is your secret ingredient. And with a loyal audience already at your fingertips, you've got a ready market for your offerings. Serve up exclusive discounts and early access to sweeten the deal for your members and watch the profits roll in.

## In Conclusion

Monetizing your membership site isn't just about making money – it's about providing value and a premium experience to your members. By mixing and matching membership fees, upselling, cross-selling, affiliate marketing, sponsored content, advertisements, and product/service launches, you can create a recipe for success that'll keep your business thriving for years to come. Just remember to keep your finger on the pulse of your audience's preferences and needs, and you'll be well on your way to turning your membership site into a money-making machine.

# Chapter 10: Scaling Your Membership Site Business

Alright, folks, it's time to take your membership site business to the next level. Scaling isn't just about growing your numbers—it's about doing it smartly, efficiently, and in a way that keeps your members happy and coming back for more. So grab a seat, because we're about to dive into the nitty-gritty of scaling your membership site like a pro.

## 1. Streamlining Processes and Operations

First things first: let's streamline those operations and get things running like a well-oiled machine.

**A. Automate Repetitive Tasks:** Say goodbye to mundane tasks like member onboarding and email marketing. It's time to let technology do the heavy lifting and free up your time for more important stuff.

**B. Delegate and Outsource:** As your workload piles up, consider bringing in some backup. Whether it's hiring virtual assistants or outsourcing content creation, delegating tasks can help you focus on the big picture.

**C. Implement Systems and Workflows:** Get organized! Developing systems and workflows ensures that everyone's on the same page and things get done the right way, every time.

## 2. Scaling Your Infrastructure

Now that we've got our house in order, it's time to beef up that infrastructure.

**A. Upgrade Hosting and Server Capacity:** Don't let your website crash under the weight of all those new members. Upgrade your hosting plan or switch to cloud hosting to handle the increased demand.

**B. Optimize Website Performance:** Speed matters! Make sure your website is lightning-fast by implementing caching mechanisms and optimizing media files.

**C. Use Content Delivery Networks (CDNs):** Spread the love! CDNs help distribute your content across the globe, ensuring speedy delivery to members no matter where they are.

## 3. Enhancing Member Engagement and Retention

Happy members, happy life. Let's keep 'em coming back for more.

**A. Expand Content Offerings:** Keep things fresh by offering a variety of content formats, from videos to webinars to downloadable resources.

**B. Implement Member Feedback Mechanisms:** Listen up! Regularly gather feedback from your members to understand what they want and how you can make their experience even better.

**C. Foster Community and Interaction:** Bring people together! Create forums, discussion boards, or social media groups where members can connect, share, and support each other.

4. **Scaling Your Marketing and Promotion Efforts**

Last but not least, let's spread the word and keep those sign-ups rolling in.

**A. Continuously Evaluate and Optimize Marketing Channels:** Don't just set it and forget it. Keep an eye on your marketing efforts and double down on what works while ditching the duds.

**B. Utilize Data Analytics:** Dive into the numbers! Use data analytics to understand member behavior and fine-tune your marketing strategies for maximum impact.

**C. Experiment with New Marketing Tactics:** Don't be afraid to mix things up. Try out new tactics like influencer collaborations or referral programs to see what sticks.

Scaling your membership site business isn't easy, but with the right strategies and a little elbow grease, you can take your business to new heights. So roll up your sleeves, get ready to hustle, and watch your membership site soar!